ALL STATIONS!
DISTRESS!

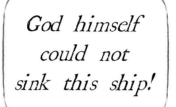

April 15, 1912:
The Day the *Titanic* Sank

ALL STATIONS!
DISTRESS!

DON BROWN

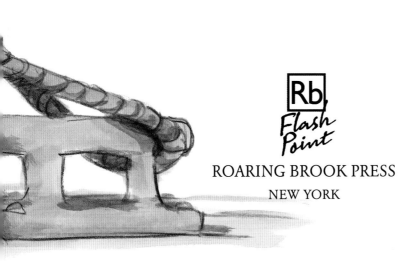

Rb
Flash Point

ROARING BROOK PRESS
NEW YORK

To Sue and David

Published by FlashPoint, an imprint of Roaring Brook Press

Roaring Brook Press is a division of Holtzbrinck Publishing Holdings Limited Partnership

175 Fifth Avenue, New York, New York 10010

www.roaringbrookpress.com

Distributed in Canada by H. B. Fenn and Company Ltd.

Library of Congress Cataloging-in-Publication Data:

Brown, Don, 1949–

All stations! distress! : April 15, 1912, the day the Titanic sank / Don Brown. – 1st ed.

p. cm.

ISBN-13: 978-1-59643-222-2   ISBN-10: 1-59643-222-5

1. Titanic (Steamship)–Juvenile literature. 2. Shipwrecks–North Atlantic Ocean–Juvenile literature. I. Title.

G530.T6B756 2008   910.9163'4–dc22   2008008934

Roaring Brook Press books are available for special promotions and premiums.

For details contact: Director of Special Markets, Holtzbrinck Publishers.

First Edition December 2008

Book design by Jennifer Browne

Printed in China

2 4 6 8 10 9 7 5 3 1

She arose beneath the skilled hands of four thousand Irish workers at Belfast's Harland & Wolff shipyard.

First came the keel and framework, the bones of the ship. Then a skin of steel deck and hull plates was attached with millions of rivets. At more than 46,328 tons, she would be the largest ship in the world. She was named Titanic.

On May 31, 1911, she slid down Slipway #3 and into the water. It took twenty-three tons of animal fat, soap, and oil to grease the slide. One hundred thousand people watched, including J. Bruce Ismay, boss of the White Star Line, the shipping company that paid for her construction. Titanic *needed more months to be fully fitted, but a ship launching is something of a birth and everyone was excited.*

No one could have guessed that she would be dead within the year.

April 14, 1912

Titanic was five days into her first voyage. She'd left England bound for New York City with about 2,200 passengers and crew. Among them were White Star's Ismay, Harland & Wolff managing director Thomas Andrews, and some of the richest and best-known people in Britain and America. The ship offered luxurious staterooms, excellent restaurants, a swimming pool, a gym, and an elegant grand staircase. She was the finest in transatlantic travel.

Still, more than half of the passengers traveled steerage,
or third class. Poor, yet ambitious, they were traveling to
America to start a new life.

By 11 PM only restless passengers and the crewmen needed to run the ship were astir. The frigid night was moonless and black, but strikingly clear. The stars burned brilliantly. The freezing sea was tabletop flat, its surface unmarked except for the crease made by the fast-steaming ship.

Lookouts Frederick Fleet and Reginald Lee stared out from the crow's nest high above the *Titanic*'s decks. They'd been told to watch out for "small ice." *Titanic*'s captain, Edward

Smith, had received warnings of icebergs from nearby ships, but he judged the threat to be unlikely. He had decided against slowing the ship before transferring command to First Officer William Murdoch and going to bed.

Fleet spied something. He sounded a three-bell alarm and then phoned the bridge, the ship's command room at the front of the top deck.

"Iceberg right ahead," he said.

Murdoch ordered a sharp turn, but a nine-hundred-foot steamship isn't a speedboat, and *Titanic* kept plowing toward the looming iceberg. Finally, she curled to port, or to the left . . . but not fast enough.

Iceberg and ship met at the starboard bow, or front right side of the *Titanic*. Fleet heard a "slight grinding noise."

First-class passenger George Harder felt a "dull thump," and then a "rumbling, scraping noise."

Mrs. J. Stuart White, another first-class passenger, didn't think much of the collision. "It was as though we went over a thousand marbles," she said.

Deep below decks, crewman Frederick Barrett had an altogether different experience. He was tending *Titanic*'s engines when suddenly an alarm sounded. A crash followed and the side of the ship tore open. Water poured in. Barrett leaped into another room but not to safety.

"A wave of green foam [came] tearing between the boilers and I jumped for the escape ladder." Barrett said.

It was the only way out. From the bridge, Murdoch had slammed shut the *Titanic*'s watertight doors immediately after the collision. The doors separated the ship's sixteen compartments. Everyone believed the closed doors would confine leaks in the hull there, leaving the rest of the ship dry. The *Titanic* could survive two flooded compartments, it was said, and on this her unsinkable reputation rested.

Captain Smith appeared on the bridge and learned they'd hit an iceberg. He called for shipbuilder Andrews. Together, the seasoned captain and the builder hurried to the bowels of the ship and calculated the damage. The flooding came from a three-hundred-foot breach in the forward hull.

Andrews knew the ship well; it was he who made the pronouncement: The blow had damaged too many of *Titanic*'s sixteen compartments. The wound was fatal. The ship was doomed. He calculated it could float for another hour and a half at best.

Captain Smith, who'd once said that modern shipbuilding designs made it impossible for him to "imagine any condition that would cause a ship to founder," must have been astonished. But whether he was or wasn't, it didn't alter his next order: Prepare the lifeboats. There were twenty, enough to carry only half the people on board.

Smith marched to the ship's radio office and told operators Jack Phillips and Harold Bride, "You had better get assistance."

The men weren't able to transmit their voices. That was still years in the future. Instead, they used Morse code, jiggling a telegraph key to make a series of clicks that represented letters. The letters had a coded meaning. They signaled:

C.Q.D. M.G.Y.

All Stations! Distress! Titanic.

It was past midnight, April 15. The ship had come to a dead stop and sank down at the bow. Distress rockets were fired skyward from her deck. Steam shrieked as it escaped *Titanic*'s boilers. Passengers, alerted by crewmen, companions, or the noise, made their way to the uppermost lifeboat deck with their life belts strapped on.

Captain Smith ordered the lifeboats loaded, shouting through a megaphone, "Women and children first!"

Neither passengers nor the crew had practiced launching the boats. When the first lifeboat was ready, there were surprisingly few passengers to board it. Despite having room for sixty-five, the lifeboat lowered away with only twenty-eight

Meanwhile, other lifeboats were readied and passengers were ordered in.

A woman begged her husband to join her in the lifeboat.

"No. I must be a gentleman," he said.

Another man promised his wife, "I'll see you later."

Many on board still believed the *Titanic* to be unsinkable and that the launching of the lifeboats was just a troublesome requirement until the ship was righted.

Families separated. There were long looks, kisses, and encouraging words.

"Be brave!"

"We'll be all right!"

"I'll look out for myself!"

Beside another lifeboat, stood the wealthy and famous owners of Macy's department store, Isidor and Ida Straus. Mrs. Straus started for the lifeboat, then returned to her husband, saying, "We have been living together for many years, and where you go I go." The lifeboat left without her. Another woman declined to abandon her husband, explaining, "We started together and, if need be, we'll finish together."

In the radio room, Phillips and Bride continued to broadcast distress signals. They even employed a newly adopted one: *SOS*. Ships replied, and one, the *Carpathia*, promised she was on her way and "coming hard." But she was several hours off.

Titanic's nose dipped lower. The sea reached open portholes and washed in.

Ismay scurried about, urging everyone to hurry. The ship's officers lowered partly filled lifeboats in the mistaken belief that hanging a full boat from the ropes was unsafe. And most went without the sailors needed to man them, crewed by whoever happened to be nearby. "I am a yachtsman and can handle a boat!" one first-class passenger volunteered and was ordered into a boat.

The decks slanted more steeply, and the sense of urgency grew. A sailor snatched one woman by the arm and another by the waist and pushed them into a lifeboat. Children were thrown in.

A woman fell between a dangling lifeboat and the side of the ship. As she plunged toward the sea, a quick-handed crewman grabbed her by the ankle.

More lifeboats dropped to the water. *Titanic*'s band played ragtime. People stumbled over huge piles of bread placed on deck by the ship's bakers as a kind of provision. A crewman tossed deck chairs into the sea thinking they might be used as rafts.

A group of men panicked and rushed a departing lifeboat. A crewman swung the boat's tiller to beat them away. Fifth Officer Lowe pulled out a revolver and fired warning shots.

Others stayed remarkably calm. One man got dressed in his finest evening clothes and proclaimed he was "prepared to go down like a gentleman."

Second Officer Charles Lightoller loaded the last large lifeboat. Straddling ship and boat, he helped women across the gap. One was the pregnant wife of passenger John Jacob Astor, one of New York City's richest men. Another woman had no life belt. A bystander removed his life jacket and handed it to her. A boy started in, but was stopped by Lightoller.

"He is only thirteen," his father argued.

"No more boys!" Lightoller grumbled, but he let him on.

Titanic's bow sank beneath the ocean's surface.

Now only four smaller lifeboats, A, B, C, and D remained. They were called collapsibles because of their folding canvas sides. Crewmen and passengers struggled to lower them off.

Unfilled collapsible D started down. On the opposite side of the ship, collapsible C was held for passengers. But despite boarding calls, it remained barely filled. Finally, with no other takers, Bruce Ismay, managing director of the White Star Line, claimed a place, and collapsible C was dropped to the sea.

The *Titanic* tilted fearsomely as its bow filled with water. The sea reached its top deck.

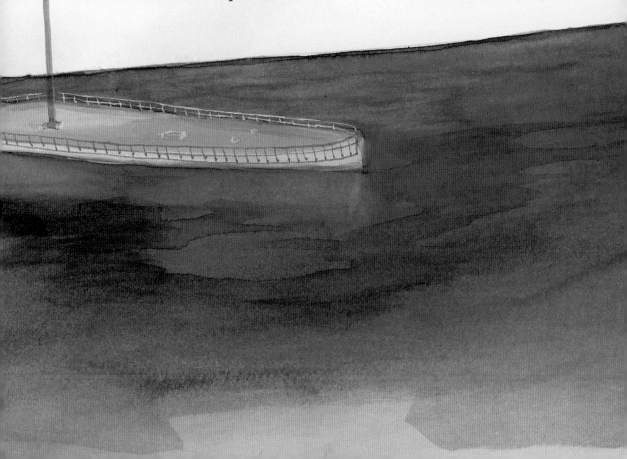

Captain Smith dashed to Phillips and Bride, still in the radio room, and said, "Men, you have done your full duty. You can do no more. Every man for himself."

But Phillips and Bride kept to their posts.

Thomas Andrews stood in a large public room and removed his life belt. A passing crewman asked, "Aren't you going to have a try for it?"

Andrews said nothing.

Water spilled into the radio room, and Phillips and Bride finally decided to quit. As they started to race out, they discovered a crewman stealing Phillips's life belt. They fought the thief for it, and left him senseless on the cabin floor.

Now a mass of people swarmed up from the lower decks. They were the poorest travelers, the third-class passengers. For no reason other than the stubborn notion that the poor shouldn't mix with the rich, not even in the face of calamity, they had been kept below. Women and children who might have found a place in partially filled lifeboats could now do nothing but try to keep their balance on the steeply angled deck.

Titanic slid deeper into the sea. A wave of water washed some people overboard and sent others scrambling toward the back of the ship.

Collapsible A went overboard and drifted free. Its canvas sides had not been unfolded and it was swamped with a foot of water. But a few lucky swimmers climbed onto it.

Collapsible B went overboard, too, with Bride holding on. Trapped for a moment underneath, he came to the surface and discovered the lifeboat had capsized. Around him, the sea was dotted with hundreds of people.

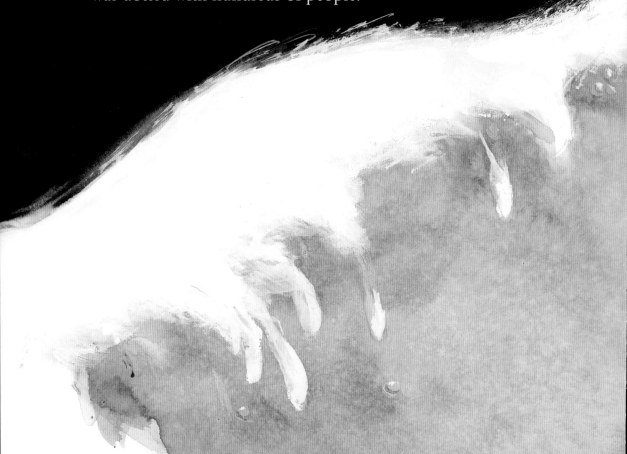

The wave sent Lightoller diving into the water, but he became trapped against the wire cover of a big ventilator shaft. The pressure of water rushing into it "glued" him to it.

"I struggled and kicked. As fast as I pushed myself off, I was irresistibly dragged back, every instant expecting the wire to go and find myself shot down into the bowels of the ship. Suddenly a terrific blast of hot air came up the shaft and blew me right away," he said.

The huge forward funnel broke off, crushing struggling swimmers, and missing Lightoller by inches. He and collapsible B washed away on the surf made by the crashing structure.

Seventeen-year-old Jack Thayer jumped feet first into the water, was sucked down, pushed up and twisted around, before coming up in the middle of wreckage.

He found collapsible B and joined Lightoller, Bride, and several others on her upside-down hull.

Titanic's lights finally blinked out. Its giant black silhouette stood out against the brilliant stars of the night sky.

"Then, the massive boilers left their beds and went thundering down with a hollow rumbling roar, carrying everything with them that stood in their way. The huge ship reared itself on end, and brought rudder and propellers clear out of the water till it assumed an absolute vertical position. She remained for a half a minute. Then she took her tragic dive," said Lightoller.

As *Titanic* became vertical, the ship's baker, Charles
Joughin, used *Titanic*'s railing as a ladder and climbed to the
rear of the ship. When she plunged, he neatly
hopped off at the water's surface,
barely wetting his hair.

It was 2:20 AM, April 15.

One hundred fifty yards away, Fifth Officer Lowe commanded five lifeboats he had strung together. When he heard the cries of the drowning, he divvied his boat's passengers among the others and then rowed back for survivors. But finding them in the darkness was nearly impossible. Only four were pulled from the sea, including a Japanese passenger adrift on a door. One of the four later died.

The occupants of the lifeboats argued about whether panicked swimmers would swarm their boats, capsize them, and drown them all. In the end, little was done. Eighteen lifeboats recovered only thirteen swimmers.

Mrs. White of New York said, "The officer who put us in the boat gave strict orders to the seamen, or the men, to make for a light. It was a boat of some kind. It was ten miles away, but we could see it distinctly. There was no doubt but that it was a boat. But we rowed and rowed and rowed, and then we all suggested that it was simply impossible for us to get to it."

Others reported seeing a ship's lights. Was it the steamer *Californian*? There's no doubt she was nearby, close enough to notice a strange ship stalled on the horizon firing rockets into the air. It was a mystery the *Californian* chose to ignore. Her engines remained off, as they had been for hours on orders of her captain, who didn't wish to navigate the ice field surrounding him.

While the *Californian* did nothing, the *Carpathia* raced around icebergs toward the *Titanic*'s position. Her captain figured he'd reach it about dawn. His crew prepared *Carpathia*

Meanwhile, in small boats on a large sea through a black night, survivors shivered. Short of men, the women took to rowing and steering the lifeboats.

"Countess Rothes stood at the tiller. Miss Swift from Brooklyn rowed every minute. Miss Young rowed every minute, except when she was throwing up, which she did six or seven times. Where would we have been if it had not been for our women?" wondered one of them.

As the night grew longer and the cold deepened, tempers shortened. Arguments grew and curses flew. One angry woman switched lifeboats. Another, Margaret Brown, was so unhappy with the crewman commanding her lifeboat that she threatened to throw him overboard and virtually took control herself.

But others had greater troubles than bickering and bad feelings. Ice-cold water lapped around the feet of the people in half-sunk collapsible A. One man constantly swung his arms to keep warm. Another froze and tumbled into the water. Those remaining shouted in unison for help until another lifeboat saved them.

Hours passed

Capsized, partly submerged, collapsible B wallowed in waves.

"We stood up in columns, two abreast, facing the bow. We maintained a balance by shifting [our] weight," Gracie said.

"Lean to the right! Stand upright! Lean to the left!" Lightoller ordered.

Toward daybreak, two lifeboats came to collapsible B's rescue. Gracie, Bride, and Charles Joughin clambered to safety. Young Jack Thayer was reunited with his mother, but cold and exhaustion prevented them from recognizing each other. Lightoller left the collapsible last, along with the body of wireless operator Phillips, who had died moments earlier.

Something flashed across the southern horizon. A boom followed.

Rockets! The *Carpathia* had arrived.

A lifeboat burned a flare. Captain Rostron of the *Carpathia* said, "I could not see the boat itself, but only the light when he showed the flare. I brought the ship to the boat. When the boat was alongside of me daylight broke, and I found [a] berg was about a quarter of a mile off."

The rosy dawn revealed an immense field of ice floes and bergs.

"We picked up [lifeboats] here and there within a range of four or five miles," Rostron said. After a fruitless search for more survivors, he steamed for New York City.

On April 18, *Titanic*'s 711 surviving crew and passengers completed their transatlantic journey, a day late and missing more than 1,500 of their original traveling companions. Among the dead were the Strauses, John Jacob Astor, Thomas Andrews, and Captain Smith. Fifty-two children died, all from the third class.

Thousands greeted the survivors, including government officials wanting to know why the "unsinkable" *Titanic* sank.

The survivors resumed their lives, some successfully, others not.

Margaret Brown's bravery and sharp wit earned her fame. Years later, a successful Broadway play and movie were staged about the feisty Mrs. Brown: *The Unsinkable Molly Brown*.

Harold Bride eventually left the wireless radio business and became a traveling salesman. Rarely did he speak of the sinking.

Archibald Gracie wrote a book about his experience. But before it was published, he died, a consequence of his ordeal.

Captain Rostron of the *Carpathia* was celebrated for his action. Captain Lord's inaction on the *Californian* sparked a controversy: Was his behavior derelict or reasonable? The argument goes on to this day.

Bruce Ismay's escape from the doomed ship became the center of a greater debate. Should he have taken one of the scarce lifeboat seats? Popular opinion of the day condemned him, and Ismay's reputation has been under a dark cloud ever since. He retired from White Star the following year and led a quiet, reclusive life ever after.

Charles Lightoller survived another sinking during military service in the First World War. He and the other surviving officers never achieved steamship commands of their own.

The White Star steamship *Titanic* remains in two pieces on the muddy seafloor, two-and-a-half miles beneath where she struck an iceberg on her maiden voyage. Though gone from view, she remains fixed on the horizon of our imagination, where she steams endlessly, haunting us.

Bibliography

Green, Rod. *Building the Titanic*. New York: Reader's Digest, 2005.

Kuntz, Tom, ed. *The Titanic Disaster Hearings*. New York: Pocket Books, 1998.

Lord, Walter. *A Night to Remember*. New York: Bantam, 1991.

——. *The Night Lives On*. New York: Avon Books, 1998.

Quinn, Paul J. *Titanic at Two*. Saco, Maine: Fantail, 1997.

Titanic Inquiry Project. http://www.titanicinquiry.org/

Titanic: Lifeboat Launching Sequence Reexamined.

   http://home.comcast.net/~bwormst/titanic/lifeboats/lifeboats.htm

Winocour, Jack, ed. *The Story of the Titanic*. New York: Dover Publications, 1960.